GROOVY COOL
WRITING TECHNIQUES

CINTA GARCIA DE LA ROSA

ISBN: 1511508906
ISBN-13: 978-1511508902

CONTENTS

DEDICATION

To the Writer.

To everyone who cannot live without pouring their
creativity onto the written page.

ACKNOWLEDGMENTS

The idea of writing these articles about writing came to me at a moment when I was suffering from the biggest writer's block ever suffered by any writer. It was awful. I wasn't able to write anything on the page and I was starting to feel so frustrated that I even thought of quitting. A writer without ideas? Come on, that's something unheard of, so if I wasn't having ideas, maybe I wasn't a writer, right? Right? It happens that I was wrong. A writer is someone who writes. Period. Even if all you write is to-do lists or journal entries. You are writing, you are a writer. So it dawned on me that maybe I just had to start writing, anything, whatever thing, and my inspiration would come back. And that's what happened.

However, I would have never put these articles, which I started publishing on my blog (http://cintascorner.com), together in book form if it weren't by the encouragement of a group of people, and I want to thank them for that, in no particular order.

First, thanks to Mark Stone, my husband, best friend, number one fan, and critic of my writing. Thank you for your encouragement, for reading my articles, for correcting my English, and for coping with my pickiness when designing my awesome cover. You know I would have never published this book if it weren't for your constant nagging about when I was going to sit down and work on it.

Thanks to Scott Bury, amazing author and editor extraordinaire, for editing my book and finding mistakes and typos where nobody else had been able to do such a thing. Thank you, Scott, for believing in my writing even in those occasions when I didn't believe in myself. It was just normal that you wrote the afterword; after all, editors always have the last word.

Thank you, Rob S. Guthrie, for being always there, in my good moments and in my bitchy moments. I would have never started a career in writing if it weren't for your valuable feedback and your encouragement. As well as with Scott, it was just normal that you wrote the foreword to this book; after all, you introduced me to this world. See what I did there? Ah, the perks of being a writer...

Thank you to Dan Leicht, a.k.a. D.e.e.L, for his constant support of my writing and for his valuable comments when he first read a draft of this book. Thanks for being there. You know that your craziness keeps me sane, if that makes sense.

Thank you to the great beta-readers, especially Irene Aprile, whose opinions helped to improve this book and who caught things that my eyes, being the author, couldn't see.

Acknowledgments

Special thanks to all the Early Readers for their invaluable opinions: Dan Leicht, Bruce Blake, Pauline Kerslake, Gary Webb, Cathryn and Lynsey Davies, Haley Keller, Ben Ditmars, Yelena Casale, Laura Pierce Francis, Kim Stapf, Linzé Brandon, Peter Germany, Alexandra Marie Brandon, Betsy Talbot, Alinka Rutkowska, and Rob S. Guthrie. Your reviews help me get better as a writer.

And thanks to you, reader, for having taken the time to pick up this little book for reading it. Let's the creativity begin!

FOREWARNING

Before you start reading this book, take into account a couple of things. I am not an expert in creative writing, so what I have written in this book are my own ideas about what works for me when I need to find more inspiration and ideas to go on writing.

The chapters are not intended to be a continuation of the previous one.

They are not related to each other, either. I am offering different techniques, and I know that maybe one may sound like a contradiction in comparison with another one, but I wrote them like that. Because I want to offer different things so we can choose from all of them.

FOREWORD

When my good friend and talented author, Cinta García de la Rosa, asked me to write the Foreword to her first non-fiction book on writing, I was honored. To have anyone ask you to become a permanent part of his or her work is a rare compliment, and I of course agreed with vigor.

However, to be forthcoming, I felt a twinge of trepidation at the same time. I have read Cinta's work in fiction, from elegant short stories, to heartwarming children's tales, to brilliantly effervescent poetry. I have always considered her one of the more talented writers I know. But just as talent teaching does not always equate to talent writing fiction, neither does an ability to write compelling, quality fiction necessarily imply the inherent skill to teach writing. It is not that I doubted my friend (after all, it was only a twinge), but it did give me pause to wonder.

As I began to read her manuscript, it took but a few pages to put any concerns I had—no matter how big or small—completely to rest. I, a writer, was hooked. In fact, one of the first thoughts I had as I read this book on our craft was that my friend was even better at teaching the process of writing than the writing itself (and as I have hopefully already convinced you, Cinta is one of the best at her profession).

I have personally spent many years toiling in writing workshops, studying in creative writing courses, and read countless books on writing—so many, in fact, that it is rare these days for me to purchase a book on the subject. It isn't that I feel I have no improvements left to make (we all have improvements left to make); what I do believe is that every artist or craftsperson reaches a point where the improvement comes mostly from the doing. We hone our skills as we work, rather than learn about them in a book.

In Cinta García de la Rosa's book, Creative Writing Techniques (Book 1), I have discovered an unexpected treasure. This is a rare book that I not only enjoyed reading, but from which I discovered I could still learn. It is the kind of book one reads many more times than once; in fact, I plan to keep a copy nearby whenever I am writing—it is that much of a compliment to any writer's toolbox.

The concept of "writer's block" has always been a tenuous one to me. In truth, I have never believed there is such a thing—I feel "writer's block" is real, but it is a symptom rather than a thing in and of itself. When we find ourselves bereft of words, staring at that cursed blank page, and nothing spills forth from our muse, I've always believed it is because of other things in our lives: distractions, stresses, emotions, and yes, even a lack of story (i.e. creativity).

Foreword

Until reading Cinta García's book, I really did not believe creativity could be summoned forth like courage, generated by exercise, or catalyzed like a chemical reaction.

I stand (or sit, rather) corrected. Creative Writing Techniques (Book 1) provides the writer with a wondrous process through which the mind forgets about whatever outside force might be causing a creative logjam. And the author does not treat the circumstance flippantly or without respect—on the contrary, what I loved so much about this book is the way its author makes you feel as if she is alongside you, journeying down the same road, offering cogent, helpful, intelligent advice (almost as if she is but whispering in your ear, coaxing you onward).

Too often I have found books that contain "writing exercises" just that: like performing calisthenics. Jumping jacks and sit-ups for the writer. Not here; not in this book. Each chapter in this book builds subtly upon the previous, as if constructing a world wherein the writer feels comfortable letting go of whatever ails him or her. By the time I finished this book, I was not only feeling more creative (and unblocked), but I found myself itching to get going again.

As I mentioned in the opening, I was honored the moment Cinta García de la Rosa invited me to write the Foreword to this book. After reading it, I am humbled as well. This is a book for writers everywhere, and of every skill level, and I am equally happy that the author will be writing another one on the subject. You can be assured I will be first in line.

- R.S. Guthrie, 2014 -

CHAPTER ONE

From Writer's Block to Writing Flow.

You are about to write. You have always loved writing and you go for it, but none of your sentences sound good. Everything you write seems to be horrible, facile, irrelevant... You delete everything and start again, but you are unable to get past the first sentence.

You have read everywhere that the first paragraph is the most important paragraph in your book, and the first sentence must hook the reader immediately. Impossible! You delete everything again.

The story was so clear in your mind, but now you can't write it down. You feel blocked. Your writing stops being something enjoyable and you lose your drive.

Has the blank page ever panicked you? Do you start writing only to feel blocked soon after you begin? Do you only write when something bad or serious happens to you? Do you think you are not creative enough? Because Franz

Kafka, Gustave Flaubert, and Thomas Mann also suffered from blank page syndrome and they were pretty successful after all.

What causes writer's block?

Writer's block comes from perfectionism, which leads us to edit while writing the first draft. This impedes the natural flow of writing. Maybe it comes from the mistaken idea that a good writer doesn't need to write drafts; if we believe that, we will get frustrated if the text is not perfect the first time.

This confuses the creative writing process with the resulting product: the novel or the story. However, writing is not a product; it's a process. And the journey for the writer is not the final destination, but the road to get to it.

The writer begins writing days before putting a word on paper or screen: that is, thinking about the text. We write even when we don't actually write. You write while researching and thinking about your ideas, and you also write long after you put down the final period, in the editing phase.

How can you prevent the blocks?

If your inner editor can't stop editing the first draft, you can do two things:

Mislead it. Write something different: poems, letters,

blog posts, journal entries. It doesn't matter what you write, as long as you write.

Take a break. Breathe, go for a walk, work out, dance, draw, read, cook, talk to friends. Do whatever your mood fancies and forget about your work in progress (WIP). Even while you are resting, your mind continues to work on your WIP, and you will see the results later. Above all, writer's block is a chance to think, a creative opportunity. If you prevent it from stopping you, it can give you a big push.

Groovy Cool Technique #1

The first creative technique to help you beat writer's block is a game we will call "IMAGINE THAT..."

Playfully speculating can mislead writer's block and open doors to creativity. To start, write down the words "What if...?" or "Why not...?", or maybe just draw a big question mark. Now the blank page won't look so empty.

Now you can start writing suppositions:

WHAT IF your page is empty because someone stole all the letters from it? What if that someone has stolen every letter from every book in the world?

WHAT IF you were a superhero whose destiny is to save the world from the disappearance of the language? What if you can only manage to save one vowel and three consonants? What if the only surviving letters are the ones in your name? Imagine that only three people in the whole world remember how to read them. What if you go on a quest to look for them? An Indiana Jones in search of the lost word?

Imagine that you aren't suffering from writer's block. Instead, it is a plague killing the letters you write as if they were ants! What if it is a divine plague - God punishing mankind for using language to tell lies? What if the Universe is using Karma to punish the world for being so chaotic?

WHAT IF an evil artist is behind the disappearance of letters because he thinks that images are more worthy than letters?

WHAT IF a group of corrupt politicians are trying to abolish the collective memory by erasing the written word?

Let's write: words die like ants crushed by the armies of men.

Imagine that someone has found the book that survived: the lost link between memory and silence. What if that book is The Odyssey? What if it is the phone book of Paris? Or the last one written by Murakami?

What if...?

CHAPTER TWO

More Pleasure, Less Stress, Relax, and Watch.

To suffer while writing is nothing new. Many artists have related inspiration to stress, even to agony: Mozart, Kafka, or Rilke, for example.

Some say that a bit of stress can help you be creative. But creativity appears when we are having fun, not when we are suffering. During the creative process, it's necessary to protect the joy of writing from your inner editor/censor. Relaxing will let you visualize ideas in a better way.

Lots of writers along the centuries have related writing to suffering, and anxiety to the process of generating and developing ideas. But what are the consequences of creative anguish? The inability to write words on a page and a lack of trust in the words you have been written down.

According to my literature classes at university, Kafka was one of the writers who suffered the most. While writing, he felt stressed and anguished, but it was even worse for him to re-read what he had written the previous day — he found it totally unacceptable. Then, he realized he had been suffering for nothing.

Such a lot of effort, stress, and anguish for nothing. Does that sound familiar to you? Have you ever felt the same?

We have all thought at some point that we don't write well enough. So we stop writing sometimes. We decide we can write later. And then we keep on postponing the creative process, although our minds don't stop working, in what we will call acts of deferral, hoping that by deferring the moment of actually writing, the words will get better. Later, we listen to the voices in our minds, but we decide those words are not good enough yet. Writer's block and deferral affect writers to the point that many artists consider anguish as an occupational hazard of the job of being a writer. Maybe you feel relieved to know that even the great Kafka felt like you do. Suffering may even seem a romantic concept to you.

Stop fooling yourself! Suffering may seem romantic, but it's not creative. The word anguish, etymologically, means to press, to suffocate, and to drown. How are we going to create anything if we feel like that? How are we going to produce ideas while feeling under pressure? To create it is necessary to flow, and that flowing state requires peace of mind, discipline, breathing, self-control, and concentration. There are certain attitudes that lead to creative effectiveness:

the right disposition and a persevering mood.

Feeling anxious while writing isn't going to help us. Not at all. We need to distinguish between:

1) The fact that anguish leads some artists to write, and

2) The fact that writing leads some artists to feeling anguished.

Now we know that the anguish we may feel while writing is the result of a wrong approach: the tendency to think that writing is an exceptional act when, in fact, it's a process. We feel anxious for not writing a single word because we have failed to identify it as the quiet stage of brewing ideas. We have called that moment writer's block when we should have recognized it as the moment when everything can happen. We tend to look for the right answer to soothe our mental anguish, but the creative personality is characterized by a tolerance of doubt and ambiguity.

It's impossible to write final drafts while writing down one thousand and one ideas; this is the moment of opening different paths. The tendency to confuse the revision stage with the creative process is what makes us suffer.

Groovy Cool Writing Technique #2

VISUALIZATION. This is a psychological exercise that consists of creating the mental image of what you want before making it real. Distance runners use it by visualizing the finish line before they start a race; chess players visualize the next several moves before they make them.

Writing is the same. First, you must relax: sit down comfortably, put your back straight, close your eyes, and take a deep breath. Pay attention to the pauses between inhaling and exhaling. Let thoughts come and go; don't try to stop and focus on them. Now visualize a character. Watch your character, free of any criticism, with your mental eyes.

Where do you see your character moving? You may see John Doe hidden in an attic; spending a day in the beach with his six brothers; attending a funeral in a tiny village; making snowballs in the city; kissing a classmate in the gym when he was ten; getting married to his girlfriend in a big church; or even singing a Taylor Swift song at a karaoke bar. You choose! It's your character! Your characters can do whatever you want them to do.

You can even use an object: an orange, for example. Imagine its color, its texture, the smell of the blossoming orange tree, the smell of the fruit, its taste... Feel it inside your mouth: the juice, the acidity, the sweetness, its touch, its wrinkled skin, the sound of your jaws while eating it, the sound of the knife peeling the orange...

You must perceive with your five senses. When you are ready, open your eyes... and write!

CHAPTER THREE

The Art of the Draft.

Writing is difficult. Always and for everybody, even for the most gifted writers. But the task gets even more difficult if we think that writing well means being good at doing just one thing; the truth is that writing well requires being really good at multitasking.

Maybe you find it difficult to come up with ideas, to organize them, to arrange them to create effective sentences, and finally put it all on the page. Maybe it's difficult for you to think of the potential reader while you write, going beyond yourself. Or maybe you don't want to show your writing to others because you are afraid of their criticism.

Those difficulties, either material or psychological, are quite diverse. However, at the bottom of every block, of every fear, is the way we were taught to write as children. School taught us to use just one half of our brain, the most logical one. The human brain has two hemispheres, right and left. Each hemisphere performs different tasks, and they complement each other. Even though we have been using mainly the left one, we need both hemispheres to write well.

When we write, we use a logical system (syntax) to create worlds (show emotions). But they contradict each other, since they are the base of two mental processes that can't happen at the same time.

How many times have you started writing a story but couldn't go past the first paragraph because you revise every sentence until you hate it? How many times have you criticized your own ideas for being bad and nonsensical during a brainstorming session?

To prevent your inner editor/censor from attacking your text while your intuitive self is still exploring ideas — to prevent the inner editor from judging or correcting at a too early stage, killing ideas or possible sentences — we must learn to write in two stages.

First, you have to let your ideas flow by writing fast; organize and revise at a later stage. Only in that way you will avoid the dreaded writer's block. School teachers taught us to love clean text, the final product, instead of valuing and loving the pleasure of the process.

Isabel Allende, one of my favorite writers, said: "Writing is like making love. Don't worry about the orgasm, just concentrate on the process."

Pour ideas onto the page at nighttime, because that's

when your logical part is more confused and tired. You will have time to correct in the morning. Or you can write by hand and revise spelling and grammar when you type it. That's how I write and, trust me, it works really well. Throw ideas horizontally on the page (as if you were drawing); you will rearrange them in a more logical, vertical way later. Write as if you were drunk so you can correct it later when you are sober and fully awake.

The left hemisphere is in charge of spelling, syntax, and the choice of the correct words in a due context. The right hemisphere is in charge of music and images, so it considers the poetic aspect of words, looks for sound, establishes relationships between words and ideas, turns emotions into rhythm...

If we want to write a poem, the rhythm of the verses is generated in the right hemisphere, but the rhyme is decided in the left hemisphere. See how we need both?

Groovy Cool Writing Technique #3

CONSECUTIVE FAST WRITING. Writing is leaping. Sometimes it's difficult to find a first sentence that can be brilliant, memorable. If you are afraid of a bad beginning, don't start at the beginning, just write! Start the page with three dots (...) and continue writing freely! Every day, write fast for 15 minutes, non-stop; speed can stun the editor you have inside.

I will share with you something that I learnt while taking a creative writing course at Oxford University. A pedagogist named Peter Elbow had great advice for everybody who wanted to be a better writer. Peter Elbow called it consecutive fast writing: write a text three times very fast in three hours.

For an hour, write fast for 45 minutes, without re-thinking. Just flow, fill the pages. Use the last 15 minutes to correct and reflect on what you wrote. In the next hour, take the central idea you developed in the first draft and rewrite everything very fast in 45 minutes; then correct again for 15 minutes. After you have thought about the third draft, you will be ready to write the fourth draft, which will become the best one.

CHAPTER FOUR

Everybody Is Creative. How to Enhance Our Creative Personality.

When you look at a blank page that insists on being blank, or after thousands of attempts to write the typical boy-meets-girl story in a more original way, I'm sure that you have also exclaimed, "I'm not creative!" And maybe you have wondered what the difference between a creative and a non-creative person is. Or maybe you want to know whether a person's personality or profession play a role in that.

I have good news for you: we are all creative. You can be creative in the kitchen, creating delicious meals. You can be creative in the artistic field, drawing beautiful pictures. You can even be creative as a homemaker, creating a wonderful and cozy home for your family. It's not all about writing.

Creativity is not a talent that only some chosen people possess and others can only envy. It's an ability and, as such, you can learn it, develop it, and use it. Everybody can learn to be creative. Don't roll your eyes, I am serious! You can do it with practice.

Every creative process has three phases: previous, conception, and subsequent. Creators usually consider the previous moment as the most important of the three. We "write" the most during the hours previous to actually putting words on paper or on screen. This is also when we can have negative thoughts about our writing ("I can't do it", "I'm not good enough") or when we can choose to postpone everything. So it's necessary for us to combine two attitudes:

Disposition. To create it is necessary to believe, to see ourselves as creative people. Only if we believe in ourselves we will be willing to create something new. When writers believe they have everything they need, the fear to fail disappears and they let themselves flow.

Avoid thoughts like "I haven't lived enough experiences," "I don't have a great imagination," "I can only speak of what I have lived," "I won't be able to catch the reader's attention"... Run away from negative thoughts! You don't need them!

We write with anxiety when we lack self-confidence: what if the challenge of the novel I have in my mind is beyond my talent? If you have those thoughts and feel stressed, please stop!

Take ten deep breaths: this will help you to relax and

find the flow your brain needs to work better with less energy. Breathe. Breathe so deep that the air gets to your belly button, helping you to find balance. Slowly.

Next, admit that everything you are looking for is inside yourself. The creative person that you are is waiting somewhere. There is a diamond in the rough you must find — a diamond that exists for sure and is called creativity.

Breathe. Trusting the creative process, your creative self, will revive your flow.

Believe in yourself: the text is a reflection of the self. Dive into the blank page like in a refreshing swimming pool on a hot day. Look for the idea that is shining at the bottom of the pool. Visualize the diamond! Repeat: "I believe in myself, I believe in my creative self". Make of that sentence your personal mantra. Breathe. Now you are in the best disposition for creating, for finding your diamond, polish it, and make it shine.

Perspiration. Creativity is not a matter of being talented, but of spending hours training to perfect this ability that we can learn. It's time to go down and work in the mine: the effort, elbows place on top of the table, eyes open 24/7, sleepless nights, the wastepaper basket filled with drafts up to the rim, the drawings, dreams captured in a notebook that rests on our bedside table, the perspiration.

Face the truth: if creativity is neither an innate gift nor a mystery, then ideas aren't going to fall from the sky like manna, and we cannot blame the muse. Making excuses and whining don't work; going down to the mine is what will work. Work hard, perspire, write, write, write, dig into your darkest thoughts.

Above all, don't blame others; we can be better or worse than others at thinking creatively, but we are talking of an ability that can be learned and acquired. Gather your courage and get to it. It's time to take control of our own creativity.

Groovy Cool Writing Technique #4

THE GAME OF THE INSOMNIAC: THE NIGHT QUESTION. You have been writing for hours, trying to reach the end of a chapter you have been in stuck for months. You don't know the choice your character should take. She has just learned that her husband, who had borrowed all her savings to open a restaurant, is having an affair with another woman. How can you go on? Before you go to bed, re-read what you have written up to then and write a specific question on a sticky note: what is my character doing with a fuel can, walking down a lonely street in the middle of the night? What is my character doing with another man, having dinner at her husband's restaurant?

Stick it to your fridge. Repeat, several times, the key question while trying to fall asleep in bed. When you wake up in the morning, before even taking a shower, before even having any breakfast or coffee (oh, yeah, I can hear your gasps of horror, but this is how it works), and before re-reading the sticky note on your fridge, write down the first thing that crosses your mind about the situation in which you were stuck. Your morning writing will have adopted a conscious approach fueled by the subconscious, which was working during your sleep.

write is le
realiॅ

CHAPTER F

Unleashing the Creative Impulse. Triggers That Shoot Ideas.

Writing often appears from intuition, igniting the desire to write even though you don't know what to say yet. The explosion that sparks creativity is a mystery, an impulse that takes place outside the language at that moment when poems and tales are born. It also unleashes a powerful force: **the creative impulse.**

Before and even during writing, we explore memory and reality until we find what we want to say and how to say it. We are moved by an unnamed desire, the pure impulse that compels us. Behind every creative impulse there is a stimulus that acts as a trigger and, before it, there is a whole world to explore and reveal to others.

The origin of the creative impulse is a mystery, for both a poet and a painter. Ideas can reach everywhere, unexpectedly, and the stimuli that lead us to them aren't always recognizable. However, the stimulus that makes us

...ss mysterious and more evident; it happens when ...y hits hard or when we go through a painful event, just ...o name a couple of examples.

Maybe you are now wondering: what happens when life doesn't hit us hard? What if life doesn't give me any reason to look for relief and comfort in writing? Then, some writers don't write; they don't need it. But some others feel that creative impulse anyway. Where do they find the strength? What is the force that makes them get up in the middle of the night to write? They are receptive people who respond to incentives. They consider that looking for the impulse and paying attention to it to discover its secrets is part of their job.

To understand the impulse as part of the job is essential. With a blank page, everything is possible if we look out the window, if we listen to the world outside and we look for things in it. The key is to listen to the impulse, to watch everything that makes it move.

We don't know the origins of the spark, but we know that its light is responsible for making us write on a café serviette what the girl at the table next to ours has just said: "I'm sick and tired of living in a pan!" It's responsible for keeping us awake in the middle of the night, scribbling a poem in the notebook we keep next to our bed. It's responsible for making us take a photograph of that young man whose hand has lost two fingers, sitting on the next park bench. And we decide to call him Jeremiah. We don't know why, but we do it.

The creative spark is responsible for making us want to write a horror story after we have been reading about that topic. Tales, novels and poems are born from a first impulse that knew how to root in our sensitivity until it takes over our will and looks for shape and sense. Not everything we scribble on a serviette will become a successful story. It can be hours or weeks before we see good words appear on the pages. Ideas may be left in stand-by for months or years; drafts stacked and forgotten in a drawer until they're ready.

Groovy Cool Writing Technique #5

I have a technique to help exploit that impulse that I call **THE FILE OF FIRST IMPULSES**.

Starting today, write down every spark, every idea that catches your attention. You are looking for an address on Google Maps and you notice the streets that run in parallel, so close yet condemned never to meet. Write it down!

Pay attention to sensorial incentives: sight, taste, touch, smell, hearing... A musician can see music in the sound of frying bacon, in the sound of an old typewriter... Those are sounds that trigger ideas. What do you see? Look! Look at the shadow of your friend on the restaurant's wall while you talk. So similar to Peter Pan's naughty shadow. And go on like that! Never stop!

CHAPTER SIX

Feeding Doubts. Some Estimating or Predicting Mechanisms.

Writing is doubting. I doubt; therefore, I write. Doubt is the fuel of storytellers and novelists, and it's always working. It never stops. Does it scare you to doubt before an empty page? Does it make you feel anxious to doubt before every intuition?

Writing is like walking cross-country: there are a lot of possibilities before us and not a single certainty. Well, whether it scares us or not, writing is born from darkness. That's where we must grab our opportunity to be creative.

In my previous chapter, we were talking about the pure impulse, and we defined it as that desire or need to write inherent to the writer's job. Now it's time to explain how every writer transforms that mysterious force, that necessary impulse, into novels and stories.

Chasing one intuition, a light in the dark, an idea, can

lead us to the story that we want to tell, even if we don't know that yet. But as we have already seen, there are different triggers, since we are all moved by different incentives. What moves us depends on our personality, so there are as many different triggers as people are in the world.

As a creator, ask yourself: what triggers your creative impulse? What mechanisms trigger your ideas? An image? An abstract image? A character? A plot? Something in the newspaper that you can't stop thinking about? Have you seen a random name somewhere and now you are trying to make up a bio for that person? Have you read an essay about fear and courage and now you can't drop the topic?

Every incentive is a good one. We have so little at the beginning — just a spark, a doubt, almost nothing! So don't belittle intuition; intuition is important, every intuition is good, no matter how small or crazy it may seem. Welcome with open arms every idea that can trigger a great story.

But stories don't find their way into your head easily. They don't evolve and shape themselves. They call from a hidden place inside your head. We have to chase those images that are waiting to be freed and turned into stories. Indeed, one of the most effective creative techniques at this embryonic stage of creation is to provoke the chasing of incentives. We need to watch, to listen, and to be sharp. We will call it SIMULATION OF AN ESTIMATING

PROCESS, and it consists of searching, searching, and searching.

Groovy Cool Writing Technique #6

So, as I have just explained, we are going to learn how to predict the creative process. To do that, we will learn how to predict with four examples.

1) **Start from a character.** You see that a woman is begging at the Tube station. She hides a mystery. She stimulates you to look for answers. The estimating has started. You start imagining that woman's past. Maybe a past that is similar to yours, but with a worse ending? Why?

2) **Start from a title.** Since today you don't know what you can write about, you start predicting possible titles until one of them triggers a story in your mind. "Organic Rubbish", you think while throwing something in the bin. "The Apple's Heart" is what you imagine while watching a woman who is eating an apple, skin and all. "Watery Feelings" is what pops in your head while watching your kid, who is about to cry. And so forth.

3) **Start from an item in the newspaper.** You are shocked when you read in the newspaper about

a murder committed by a famous person. You stare at the picture: that arrogant yet scared look. Can you imagine what a famous person would feel when suddenly being despised by everybody?

Start from a focus. Sometimes it's just a gesture, a movement, a certain action. It's like seeing a single detail surrounded by a cloud; little by little, you discover the owner of that shaking finger, or which body performs that harmonious movement, or who the owner of the emerald earring hanging from that earlobe is.

CHAPTER SEVEN

Are You a Good Observer? The Two Cameras and The Swinging Look.

Like a castaway who sends signals from his deserted island, the writer's messages are preserved in a book and then thrown into the ocean.

By now, we all know that we don't start a book by writing, but by exploring the island and planning how to get off. In order to have something to write about, writers must fill themselves with tales, words, and experiences. Look, listen, be quiet! Record everything by using your two cameras, so later on you just have to write.

It is impossible to be a good speaker if you haven't learnt how to be a good listener, in the same way as it is impossible to cook a good meal if you don't know what to do with the ingredients. To learn how to give, first you need to learn how to receive. To learn to write, first you need to read everything that surrounds you. We write from what we have lived, seen, heard, and felt in the world. So, the more open we are, the more receptive we are, the more creative opportunities we will find along the way. The writer opens doors, discovers what is on the other side, stores every incentive observed and lived, and later on plays and works with them.

Before writing, you must turn your personal radar on and make it work full time. The "writer's camera" functions manually, it doesn't work consciously, and it moves all the time in every direction: it spins, shifts from side to side, varies the focus...

We will add a very important nuance to the wise saying "writing is looking"; from now on we will say that "writing is the swinging look".

Maybe you think that you are already an observer, and surely you are. But we don't all look at the same things or in the same way:

> 1) Are you one of those writers who sits on a bench to see possible characters pass by, drawing sketches of their faces and demeanours? That woman in a red coat and trainers, that old man walking with a cane who has bumped into a tourist who was roller-skating, those two shop assistants in jeans who are smoking in front of their shop at ten o'clock in the morning. Emily Dickinson said, "The possible's slow fuse is lit by the Imagination."

What if the old man with the stick is an experienced, retired pickpocketer who, after bumping into him, has stolen the young skater's wallet, and uses the stolen money to buy a nice dress for his granddaughter at the shop where the two girls in jeans work?

2) Are you one of those writers who sit on a Tube seat and start scribbling thoughts in that notebook you always carry with you? Do you sometimes concentrate on your writing so much that you miss your stop? Or maybe when you read a book you underline those sentences that seem to be talking about you? You write, "I feel blue today". And once more your imagination lights the fuse. I am like... an apple that has been bitten all over except for the core, being exposed to the world, getting rusty when touched by the air, and being finally thrown away.

If you identify yourself with the first type of writer, your camera is on external mode. You are interested in the outside world and its anecdotes. You walk the streets paying attention to every little detail, you have a good orientation when you go to a new city, you discover possible characters and make up possible events for them. You like action films, novels with external conflicts, TV shows that challenge you to discover who the murderer is. You have a tendency to write using the third person narrator. Maybe you like playing to search for the seven differences out of two almost identical images.

If you identify yourself with type two, your camera is on internal mode. In this case, you walk the streets while singing your favorite song, or reciting your latest poem; you don't pay attention to your surroundings, since you normally walk while looking down or while reading a book. You are connected to what happens inside yourself, including your physical feelings; you are aware of your feelings and emotions, and you know how to express them. You like movies with a psychological plot, intimate novels, poetry and essays. You tend to write using the first person narrator. Maybe you like reading your daily horoscope.

But be careful! Making up a story is creating a whole world, so you must be able to make the events vivid enough for the reader's enjoyment. You can't tell the events as if you were writing for a newspaper. Narrators don't tell stories; they transmit them. We pass on experiences. That needs observation that swings back and forth from internal to external. If you only look outside and it's very difficult for you to connect with feelings, how are you going to know how that retired man feels while stealing the wallet? If you only look inside, how are you going to put those feelings in a body with limbs, and that body in a street, and that street in a city, and that city in the nineteenth century? Facts without feeling create a lifeless story. There are feelings in both E.T. and Snow White. We can't tell without moving. But feelings without facts can't be shared, can't be told, can't be seen.

So, when you write... swing! Even if you are more interested in external (type one) or internal (type two) plots, you need to find the balance at some point. What does the weather today say about my character's mood? Is it cold like his thoughts? What is the woman in the red coat thinking? Does she feel like a half-eaten apple with a rusty core? We link about what happens inside and what happens outside by using lateral thinking, by the association of ideas, thanks to our right hemisphere. If swinging is hard for you, you can develop your ability to do it by playing at communicating vessels.

Groovy Cool Writing Technique #7

COMMUNICATING VESSELS: THE TECHNIQUE OF IDENTIFICATION TEN PER TEN. Make a list of ten random objects, the first ones you can see from your desk: pencil, window, hard drive, fireplace, telephone, calendar, heater, dictionary, door, ink. Look for the communicating vessel between you and a pencil, between you and a window... Like the pencil, you also get consumed. Like the window, you open and close too.

Let's make things a bit more difficult. Don't complain, because nobody said that this was going to be easy.

However, I hope that it is enjoyable and useful. Make a list of ten words quite far from your experience. You can use a dictionary to help you if you want: iceberg, trombone, top hat, deer, Viking, helicopter, sword, pipe, astronaut... Like the iceberg, you also hide a part of you. Like the trombone, you are also too big to sound sweet. And you can continue like this with the rest of elements.

What if we link in the same story a pencil and an iceberg, a window and an astronaut? Things that are close to us with things that are far away? I see a pencil, stuck by a child into an iceberg made of mashed potatoes, which he doesn't want to eat at his school cafeteria, while he looks out of the window and dreams of becoming an astronaut... until he discovers that the moon is made of mashed potatoes! Yuck!

Now you go on...

CHAPTER EIGHT

The Creative Memory. Exploring Memory Lane.

To create means "to bring into existence something that didn't exist before". But that something must be valuable. We can create a misunderstanding out of thin air, but that doesn't turn us into creative people. What role can memory play in our goal of being innovative?

In the previous chapter, we talked about observation as the starting point for any creation: novels, tales, and poems are born from feelings and events observed from our own particular perspective, whether we look inside or outside ourselves. Nonetheless, if we are dealing with novelties, you may ask yourself: is it only the new that matters? Only this anguished feeling that is crushing me right now? Only the dialogue that is happening at the kiosk, right before my eyes on this Sunday while I buy the newspaper?

When we talk about the necessity of being innovative while writing, we can think that the creation of a text always happens from what we observe onwards; we have to start from where we lived today and go on inventing while walking towards our tomorrow.

Wrong. Totally and absolutely wrong. Wrong in a non-groovy-cool way. And this book is about groovy cool techniques.

The fact is that we should be looking back. What about you? Do you travel through your memories? How good is your retrospective look? Memory seems to be the opposite of creation, but that's a false impression. We can get great creative benefits and new approaches by exercising our memory.

We write from our experience, both endogenous and exogenous, from what we observe inside and outside. Looking inwards also includes looking at our memories, the past, what we have already lived, even what we thought that we had forgotten but is still alive in our subconscious.

If you want to write, starting to observe from now on won't be enough. You also need to look inside yourself. Dust off all those archived memories; they are a powerful and really groovy source of ideas and inspiration.

Turning inwards, immersing in your feelings... For the poet, memories are very important, and childhood is a never-ending source. We can compare memory to a big library with different sections. It's important to keep our library tidy, to know how to categorize the materials, where we store memories in our library.

Do you know the treasures you keep in your memory? On which shelf? Our mental library has three floors:

1) **Immediate or sensory memory.** We perceive everything with our five senses and we remember those things thanks to our sensory memory. So this is the first floor in our library. It is automatic (everything that we perceive is stored) and very fragile (those memories are deleted after ten minutes). In a real library, this floor would be the one devoted to daily newspapers, magazines, and ephemeral publications. Has anybody ever asked you what you had for lunch the previous day, but you couldn't remember what you ate? This is the kind of memory we are talking about here. Even so, sometimes we remember feelings with great accuracy after a long time; we get detailed, almost photographic images. For some reason, those feelings refuse to be forgotten, just like that piece of news that you cut out of a newspaper more than twenty years ago and still keep in a drawer. The sensory stimuli that get more attention from us go straight up to the second floor of our library and become a part of the short-term memory.

2) **Short-term memory.** This kind of memory is working memory. It's a temporary memory

with low capacity for retention that only lasts while we are doing a specific task. When we stop doing that task, that memory disappears little by little. Maybe you learnt how to cook lentil soup while you were living with your parents long time ago, and you cooked it a million times. But when you moved to your own house, you stopped cooking lentil soup. If someone asks you to cook it now, you would probably need to look for the recipe. This floor of our memory is like the library floor where the study rooms are and where you can borrow books. It is also the memory that helps us to remember words by association, either because they rhyme or because we have developed a system to remember them. Imagine a father with nine daughters, who calls them in alphabetical order so he can remember all their names.

3) **Long-term memory.** On this floor, we archive memories of events that happened a long time ago, and they are archived by categories. It happens in the same way with more recent memories, but they are prone to be forgotten. It is here where a writer takes the plunge: the more we observe, the more we retain; therefore, the more significative the memories. We are in

the area of the incunabula, in the attic, the top floor of our library. There is where the episodic memory works, storing our life events, which are of the utmost importance for the writer. Can you recall your furthest childhood memory? The most beautiful one? Without this episodic memory, we would forget that we have to go back to work on Mondays, we wouldn't be sure whether we have turned the stove off, and we wouldn't have evocation powers! That would be a disaster for a writer! (Oh, no! Run for your lives!)

We have two groovy cool creative writing techniques we can use to deal with our memories and make them work for our creative writing in this chapter.

Groovy Cool Writing Technique #8

Linking memories from the past to the present. Reach for your furthest memory: your father lifting you up to place the star on top of the Christmas tree, for example. That memory takes you to that day when your father lifted you up into a tree during a picnic for your tenth birthday. That tree leads you to another tree in summer camp, when you fell from the swings, chipping one of your teeth and making the boy you had a crush on laugh. It made you feel as upset as when your friend Jocelyn laughed at you when your teacher caught you cheating on a Latin exam... Continue!

Groovy Cool Writing Technique #9

Drawing your family tree. Graphically visualizing and retaining the story of your ancestors can help a lot to keep your memory fully awake. Do you know the maiden name of your grandmother? Do you know whether any of your relatives went to war? Did any of them lose their spouse and get married again? Maybe you belong to that new branch of the family. Do you know secrets about your family worth of getting turned into a novel? Write them down, don't let the memories disappear. Every writer creates pages to avoid oblivion.

CHAPTER NINE

Creativity on a Surface. Writing in Line.

Writing is putting down one word after another, but thoughts neither pop into our heads in a line, nor is the world reduced to just one dimension.

What we casually call outlining ideas implies reducing a multidimensional reality to the linearity of the written word. But how can we fit a whole world into a nutshell? How can we make a waterfall go through a funnel without losing its strength? Once more, the answer is in our brain. We need to learn how to organize our thoughts in a creative way.

Maybe you have felt sometimes that you have plenty of ideas but you are unable to channel so much information. How can you turn the hodgepodge of thoughts you have in your head into the thinnest thread? Or even better, how can you slow down your train of thoughts to make it compatible with the much slower pace of writing? In this respect, making cinema is easier because the screen allows the director to create and, at the same time, it allows the spectator to experience, at once, the personality traits of the character, the setting in which the action takes place, the music that provides the scene with a suitable atmosphere, the words uttered by the characters...

3, 2, 1, action! A young witch stands in a library, surrounded by very tall bookshelves. She is alone in the dark, reading with the aid of a candle while we listen to Debussy's music and the girl whispering "mandrake!" All of that jumps to our eyes thanks to the screen! On the other hand, the writer cannot describe that multiple reality in a simultaneous way. The writer can only put one word after another, choosing which one goes first and which one goes next. We can write "witch" first or maybe "library"? We can write one or the other, but not the two at the same time. That's how it works. Despite that, successful writing requires that the writer depict the whole of the world.

One of the biggest limitations a writer must overcome is the linearity of writing. An artificial linearity, since our brains naturally treat information in a global and simultaneous way: relating ideas and connecting images, concepts, and feelings in a meaningful way.

The world is spherical, but writing is flat, so what to do? We don't want our writing to be flat. So how can we write a novel that transmits the power of the events even though we have pushed them through the sieve of writing? How can we prevent linearity from killing our thoughts? How can we prevent ideas from dying on the page, turned into a sad listing or a summary? That's why the job of writer is so difficult: it requires pushing a tornado through a keyhole without reducing it to a mere breeze.

Writing fiction is not the same as writing a composition. At school, we were taught to redact, to put information in a line, to make sketches to organize that information in a logical way. That allows us to put ideas in order, from the plan to the conclusion, but it doesn't allow to relate ideas in a parallel way. Writing literature isn't listing, but connecting, because everything is connected in the real world. We write to show possible, whole, complex, and related worlds. We suggest a relationship between the character's strength and the wild landscape, or between the rain and sadness, but it doesn't seem possible to say everything in parallel at the same time...

When confronting this challenge, the answers are in our brain, especially in the right side, the creative part of our brain. While the left hemisphere deals with the information in a logical way — we learnt how to use it at school — the right side deals with the information in a global way, since it links all our thoughts like a blender. It is going to be very useful for you as a writer to think in two ways, using both parts of the brain in succession: channeling your thoughts on a surface before you do that in line.

Let's put into practice what we have learnt so far...

Groovy Cool Writing Technique #10

THROW WORDS TO THE WIND. Take isolated words and sow them not in lands that have been already exhausted, but in fertile land where you can work with them. Be original! Write words on a page, not connected in sentences, without using any syntax. Spread all over the page, not one after the other. Diverse, scattered, like seeds in the wind: dice, dart, banana, fish... Often you will find that you have written related words closer together; you will have grouped them together either because they are similar or contrary. Dice and dart shared their initial letter, and they also have opposite meanings: a dart aims to a bullseye or an objective, but a dice has no aim or object since it just depends on luck. Write isolated words and link them with a spider web in a first draft; you will put them in sentences later.

Groovy Cool Writing Technique #11

DRAW IDEAS. Look, draw and write, in that order. Let the right hemisphere of your brain draw an image of what you want to say. Look at the world first, then draw your thoughts. What did you get? Horns? A lush tree? Write from that image. You can also visualize a picture and see where it takes you. You can even outline ideas, drawing graphics when the linearity of a text is too limiting, and sketching tables of what you had previously written.

Groovy Cool Writing Technique #12

BLAH, BLAH, BLAH... Speak the text out loud before writing it down. Use your mobile phone to record whatever idea you have in your mind. Just talk without stopping, without deleting. When we talk, we transform complex thoughts into linear sentences at a very high speed. That immediacy stuns the left hemisphere of our brain, so that's the moment when our right hemisphere can work freely. Talk. The trick is doing it very quickly, without caring about coherence or cohesion. You can give coherence to those ideas at a later stage.

CHAPTER TEN

In People's Shoes. If You Want to Write, Empathize!

Narrating requires creating realistic worlds, as well as vehicles that can transport the readers to those worlds and reflect both the reader's and the characters' emotions. Narrating is not only telling the facts, but also passing on the feelings that those facts evoke. Passing on, infecting, transmitting feelings as if they are a virus. We don't have to convince with arguments; we have to move the reader with feelings. To do that, we must understand our own rationality as well as others', and we have to find a way to use all that understanding in a creative way. How? By feeling the story as a whole, through the empathy principle.

Imagine that you are about to write a story about two unemployed flat-mates who have totally different concepts about honesty. To show that, you place them in a supermarket with just a $10 note. One of them buys cheap things: mac n' cheese, ketchup, a loaf of bread, and even though he is dying for some beer, he doesn't get it because he is on a low budget. The other one, without anybody noticing, hides inside his jacket a small and very expensive imported piece of cheese.

Character 1 acts according to what he thinks is the decent, reasonable and best thing to do according to the world's rules (We shouldn't steal). Character 2, on the other hand, acts according to what he thinks is the decent, reasonable and best thing to do according to his own rules (This world is against young people, not offering us a job... I owe myself something that I am craving... Anyway, this cheese manufacturer exploits its workers... I am stealing from the rich to feed the poor, so I am Robin Hood...).

As the author, do you agree with Character 1 or with Character 2? Would you be able to transmit the feelings of each of your characters to your readers without praising or condemning them, without showing your position, without taking sides or judging?

Building a story is getting to know and to love every one of your characters. It is becoming every one of the items and landscapes that comprise your story. In order to talk about a topic, the writer will need to **master that topic** during the exploration of the materials, in the researching stage, long before writing a single line. Yes, I said "master that topic", because you cannot stay in the shallow part of the pool; you need to dive into the deepest part of that problem and understand the whole of it. Only in that way will your story be interesting and will you as an author be able to give your readers an active role in it. If you want to write, it won't be enough if you get involved in the story only from one point of view. It won't be enough if you just sympathize with the situation, either. It will be necessary that you feel **empathy** with the situation you are narrating.

Empathy and creativity.

Experts are always talking about different principles that can help writers to develop their craft. My professors of literature and creative writing at university liked to name them from time to time, but sometimes I forget how to use them, or I use them without being fully aware that I am doing so. Probably, the same happens to you, too.

What are these basic principles of the creative process?

The Empathy principle: not really a principle of the creative process, but one trait of a creative person — the ability to identify both mentally and affectionately with other people's feelings as if they were his or her own.

The Abundance principle: both in nature and in creativity, it is necessary to propose many, many suggestions in the hope that at least one of them survives. For example, think of how many spermatozoids are needed so only one can reach the desired goal. The same happens with ideas: you need to generate a lot of ideas so at least one of them can find the fertile path to success.

The Flexible principle: creativity needs mental flexibility, running away from rigid opinions, looking inside ourselves for a second self, knowing and valuing that duality, and valuing the group inside our mind.

The Complexity principle: an incident is never an isolated incident, but a whole bunch of incidents, depending on the point of view, depending on the who saw it, where it happened, and the mood we were when contemplating it.

The Agreement principle: also called Validity Principle, it reminds us that creativity prefers realism to truth, that there is not only one truth but many, and that creating is finding an agreement among all those valid truths.

Go back to your story about the flat-mates in the supermarket. To write it, you have to search for both Character 1 and Character 2 inside yourself. Look for that plurality, that doubt, those thoughts, that contradiction. You have all those things inside. Just let them out.

What is the idea of honesty to the supermarket's cashier? What about the old lady who always tries to jump the queue?

Now look for some unusual witness: what does the blueberry jam jar think about what Character 2 is doing while it contemplates the scene from one of the shelves? Does the jam jar dream of being stolen? Does the jam jar fear Character 2? Why? Taking blueberries out of the bush is not a crime, so why would it be a crime to take a piece of cheese?

Have you ever considered the point of view of the rear wheel of the shopping cart that spins contrary to the others, as if it were trying to divert the other three from the right way? Is our Character 2 that misplaced wheel that tries to create a new morality by breaking the established rules — if the world is ripping off the person, why isn't the person going to rip the world off? What if you write your story from that alternative point of view?

What does the little piece of cheese think of all this while hidden in Character 2's pocket?

What will happen when we keep on writing this story and, at a certain point, the two young men must compete with each other for a job, or for a woman's love, or something equally valuable? Will their opposite ideas about honesty jeopardize their friendship?

Looking at the story from unbelievable and unexpected points of view while considering different truths that are valid for this problem is what beautifies the creative process and enhances the possibilities of our story. If you want to learn more about empathy and its application to the creative text, you should watch Blade Runner, a great movie based on the novel Do Androids Dream of Electric Sheep? By Philip K. Dick. If you don't want the characters of your stories look like androids or replicates, you must step into their shoes, crawl under their skins — you must empathize with all of them, and you need to do all of these with that cleverness necessary for being a good novelist and storyteller. The only answer to the question "what's the real meaning of the word TREE?" is "according to whom?"

Groovy Cool Writing Technique #13

EMPATHETIC DEFINITION. Define tree from the point of view of a bird, a plane, a tourist, a hanged man, a prisoner, traffic lights, a parachutist, an arsonist, a woodcutter, a mushroom, an apple, a star, a nearby tree, a pencil, a table...

Now define tree while you are feeling in love, angry, sad, shameful, generous, scared...

CHAPTER ELEVEN

Magical Artefacts and Creativity.

Are you looking for new ideas for a plot?

We are in Chapter 11 — can you believe we made it this far? Well, by now I think that you have learned enough about the creative process as to know that everything is fair in the first stage of creation, the stage of research and imagination. You must allow yourself to let go and ignore that naughty inner editor that likes to spoil the fun before it has even started.

Also ignore the limiting tendency to solve matters quickly, and any preconceived ideas about what is normal, ordinary, acceptable, and realistic. Today, we will look for inspiration in the extraordinary, fantastic, supernatural, impossible, absurd, and wonderful.

An English doctor named Wilfred Trotter once said, "The mind likes a strange idea as little as the body likes a strange protein and resists it with similar energy. It would not perhaps be too fanciful to say that a new idea is the most quickly acting antigen known to science. If we watch ourselves honestly, we shall often find that we have begun to argue against a new idea even before it was completely stated."

He was so right! We believe that the fact of opening to new possibilities, to new realities, is a way of losing control, so we struggle to remain in charge, even though we know that only by letting go can we find something new.

There is an old saying that states, "If you don't like where you are, move." That resistance to new ideas especially affects us when we want to write: we want new things, of course, but we don't want to move. If we only stay in our comfort zone, do we really want to continue doing what we always do? Forever?

We look for new stories in our daily lives, our friends' lives, in the news on TV or in the newspapers. We complain about the same-old same-old. Can it be that we undervalue imagination and fantasy as literary tools? Maybe an unconscious prejudice makes us think that fantasy and magical things are just childish, not very important things that only interest to children.

Question the origin of that fierce defense of reality. Maybe it makes us feel safer to deal with what we already know. Maybe it is sheer laziness. I have been in several creative writing courses organized by Oxford University

(UK) and, in all of them, there was always one student who, after being told that their stories and characters lacked authenticity, would snap: "How can it lack authenticity if it is about me, if that story happened to me?"

I hope you are rolling your eyes, dear reader, because I rolled my eyes so much when I heard that, I thought my eyeballs would get stuck inside my head. "You saw how your handbag sank into a lake and then you found it, soaking wet, in your living room? Yeah, right..." Don't feel ashamed for having a huge imagination or for admitting that what you are making up seems totally absurd and unlikely to happen in real life. Because, let's face it, sometimes the boundaries between realism and fantasy is not clear. Is Alice in Wonderland a fantasy book when, after all, it seems quite logical that those wonders happen while Alice is sleeping and they end once she wakes up? There are some medieval books about making pacts with the Devil; those books reflect a reality that was possible according to the medieval reader, but highly fantastical for readers nowadays.

Today we perceive reality differently than do Jules Verne's first readers or Blade Runner's first watchers. So, don't let the present reality restrict your stories — and project them toward the future, toward the hypothetical reader!

The writer is a creative child who plays. OK then: let's play like what we are, creative children, by following the rules of fantasy. Do you know who Vladimir Propp was? No? Shame on you! Nah, really... Vladimir Propp was a linguist who decided to analyze popular Russian tales back in 1928. Propp paid a lot of attention to the study of the characters and he listed the seven most frequent roles:

1) the hero or searcher (the protagonist)

2) the king (the authority)

3) the princess who is in love with the hero (the reward)

4) the false hero (the one who will take advantage of any situation in order to get some benefit)

5) the aggressor (the antagonist)

6) the donor (a friend or collaborator who helps the hero)

7) the magical helper (an object, bit of advice, or skill that the hero possesses).

I am sure that you can match those roles with any familiar faces from your favorite fantasy stories. Indiana Jones is the hero, the **searcher** (looking for the Holy Grail, the Lost Ark...). Frodo, the Hobbit, is a **hero** in The Lord of the Rings; who is accompanied by the perfect **donor,** his friend Sam; who carries a **magical helper,** the One Ring; and who has to face the **antagonist,** Sauron.

The **aggressor** or antagonist of Harry Potter is

Voldemort, and the **authority** is Dumbledore. Harry also can count on two extraordinary donors, Ron and Hermione, and the magical helpers that normally go with a wizard.

Do you remember any **false heros**? In The Lord of the Rings, Saruman says that he is going to war as an ally, but indeed he wants to gain power by force. Gollum claims to be looking for a safe shortcut for the Hobbits when he was really leading them toward the spider.

Groovy Cool Writing Technique #14

FANTASISE WITH YOUR STORIES. Choose an **extraordinary skill** for your hero. For example: he can live without eating; he can summon rain and thunder; he can talk to animals; he can make up and tell fascinating stories... Now choose for your antagonist an auxiliary magical object: a mobile phone with X-rays, a fountain pen that houses a muse; a hat that was stolen from an astrophysicist and that keeps the brilliant ideas of its former owner; a magic ball that lets you see alternative pasts, so you can know what would have happened if...

Now try to situate both the hero and the antagonist in a story and make them deal with a conflict: John is a writer with the ability to tell fascinating children tales who, after his son's death, has lost his creativity and has run out of ideas. Pressured by his publishers (the authority) and by his wife (the princess), he becomes an alcoholic. In a writers' conference, drunk in the bar, he meets the new promising writer of fantasy books who has absolutely outsold him. She is a mysterious woman named Sena, who is the owner of a magical artefact: a fountain pen that houses a muse. When she puts the pen to the paper, wonderful stories flow from it. John will try to get that fountain pen whatever the cost. But when he gets the wonderful pen, he discovers that the ink it uses it is not real ink, but human blood — the blood of children Sena has murdered. Childish blood pours onto the pages of the evil author to re-create the dreams and fantasies of the children she has killed. When will John discover all this? After stealing the fountain pen following a night of passion with Sena at the hotel? Or when he starts writing with the pen and starts describing the biggest dream of his son, who died under mysterious circumstances?

CHAPTER TWELVE

The Limiting Effect or the Power of the First Time.

A novel is made of words written one after the other. Writing is like going on a journey: everything starts with a first step.

What happens when we are unable to take that first step? Sometimes we fall into the trap of our own perceptions, which are not able to bring together the right-now with the long-term benefits. Sometimes, in order to defeat the dreaded writer's block, that panic we fear when facing the blank page, we need to overcome a small obstacle situated at the beginning of the creative process: the so-called **"limiting effect"**.

When you were a teenager, you smoked that first cigarette because you wanted to look grown-up and cool in front of your friends. With the passing of time, you may have tried to quit smoking so many times, but failed and wished you had never started that habit. That, my dear friends, is what we call **positive limiting effect**: we start doing something, and create a habit because that first step is something nice and easy, and then we cannot avoid the bad consequences of our poor decision.

When we are about to start writing, it's more common that the contrary happens: we wish to create something wonderful, but we can't because the first step is a very difficult one. That's the **negative limiting effect**. It could lead us to decide to postpone what we love doing, of our thinking "I will write tomorrow," procrastinating even though the only thing that we want to do is to write.

In that case, ask yourself if you are one of those people who don't face that new project that has been lingering in your mind just because you are afraid of taking that first step? You know that, once you start, the story will flow easily, but you struggle with those first paragraphs. You are full of doubts and uncertainties that make you wonder whether you are as good a writer as you think. That's why you postpone the moment of sitting in front of the computer or the notebook: you are trying not to suffer, even if it is just temporary. And that's how you prevent something as wonderful as a novel or a story.

Are you the kind of writer who never participates in a literary contest just because taking that first step is something quite emotionally difficult for you? Maybe publishing your collection of poems depends on your meeting certain people or talking to them on the phone, but you feel too shy to do that? Writing and publishing requires time to organize the text, revise, edit, proofread, print, make photocopies, and distribute query letters with your manuscript; you need to overcome that resistance that proceeds from the fear of failure or rejection.

If you want to write, just write! If you want to participate in a literary contest, just submit your writing! If you want to publish a collection or anthology, call whomever can help you with that!

It is of the utmost importance to prevent the negative limiting effect: **the personal perception is limited and it tricks us by presenting a small initial blockage as an insurmountable mountain.** Beware the mirage! Remember that every journey starts with a first step; if you cannot take that little first step, the rest doesn't matter.

I am sure that you are thinking by now that advising is easy but overcoming that initial creative block is not. What can we do so we don't give up when facing a small obstacle? Once more, the answer is in your creativity. Let's practice some techniques that can help you to divert your negativity and start writing.

Groovy Cool Writing Technique #15

FIRST TIMES. The positive limiting effect is the trigger of many stories. Literature is packed with "first times" that lead to a whole series of calamities. What if your main character were the victim of the positive limiting effect? For example, your protagonist steals ten euros from her grandma's purse because she knows that the old lady keeps her money in her top first drawer and that her memory is not the same as it was years ago. The first step is very easy because it is tempting but, in the long term, it will have bad consequences.

Let's go a bit further. What if the girl's mother doesn't believe the old lady because she thinks that her memory is failing and more probably she put the money somewhere else? What if the mother thinks that it was the cleaning lady who took the money, and fires her? What about the granddaughter? Do we know what she wanted the money for?

Let's consider a different example. Imagine you are writing about a character who plays a slot machine for the first time and wins the jackpot. Or maybe you are writing about a character who had sex for money once but now can't leave that world? What about a character who takes drugs because someone invited him to try them and now can't stop?

In Guy de Maupassant's The Diary of a Madman, the main character is a magistrate who becomes addicted to murdering because the first step (killing a bird as rehearsal) was very easy for him (apart from "atrocious and delightful"), and then he just can't stop killing people. He will murder children and adults alike for years, feeling untouchable thanks to his job, and he will live until the end of his life being respected by everybody without ever being punished for his horrible acts.

Now think of a positive limiting effect for the main character in your next story, so it can serve as the trigger for the rest of the story. Try not to think of something typical, like gambling, drugs, or sex. Do as Maupassant and go beyond what is expected. He answers the question: what is the positive limiting effect for a mad person? There is a lot of inventiveness in his idea, since the limiting effect in a mad person is not the same as for any other person. His character finds it as easy to kill a bird as any other person finds it is easy to step on an ant.

Now imagine that your main character is a university professor who plagiarizes a brilliant student's essay. From that moment on, he can't stop plagiarizing and he even plagiarizes classic authors.

The first lie between a couple is the easiest one — so easy that we may even not notice. Sometimes it is easier than saying the truth. But lying causes a series of problems that can lead to the end of the relationship. What if the first lie between a man and a woman triggers the plot of your next novel?

Groovy Cool Writing Technique #16

WORD SHAKER. Draw on a page a table with seven columns, like the one you see below. Combine the words in each column to find the first sentence of your next story. Just take one word from each column and create a sentence. Come on! Be creative!

ADJECTIVES	NOUNS	VERBS	ADVERBS	NOUNS	PREPOSITIONS	NOUNS
Vulgar	Winter	Hide	Soon	Drawing	Of	Generosity
Defeated	Judge	Procreate	Silently	Chameleon	On	Courage
Bright	Treasure	Promise	Unwillingly	Picture	For	Light
Tiny	God	Captivate	Far	Bill	Without	Landscape
Empty	Slave	Provoke	Quietly	Day	Before	Sense
Blue	Evil	Grow	Yesterday	Caress	Behind	Passion
Sleepy	Cart	Cause	Step by step	Grain	Between	Ostrich
Distant	Neighbor	Shoot	Today	Death	With	Pause
Blind	Lover	Remember	Strongly	Poor	Against	Snow
Stubborn	Drawer	Remain	Slowly	Kindness	From	Sand

CHAPTER THIRTEEN

Filling Notebooks. Feeling Curious Like Leonardo da Vinci.

Every creative mind explores and asks questions about reality. What's the difference between the mind of a great genius like Leonardo Da Vinci and the creative mind of a person like you or me? The only difference is the quality of the questions. Don't worry. You can expand your ability to make up stories by improving your ability to ask good questions. How? Having an open mind and attitude, and looking inside yourself for those creative triggers that shoot amazing ideas. Leonardo Da Vinci used to take a notebook with him at all times, so he could write down everything that came to his mind: sketches, thoughts, ideas...

Writing a personal diary offers only advantages for our development as writers. Against the obstacle we perceive on the blank page, against procrastination, keeping a diary allows automatic and fluid writing whose main function is to exteriorize feelings and to vent frustrations. Many famous writers have used the diary as a means to keep on writing every day: Franz Kafka, Anne Frank, Anaïs Nin, and many others.

Keeping a diary allows you to let go, transmit, and flow. However, all too often, we don't write in our diaries every day, as the term implies. We turn to our diaries on those days when something painful happens so we can pour out our feelings, and we forget about our diaries on happier days. If you think that a diary is too old-fashioned for you, write a blog instead. Imagine that! I just solved your problem. You are welcome.

For those who prefer to write on a real diary, one that you can touch, hug, stroke, and even take to bed, I will tell you how to fill the pages of that notebook in a way that will keep you company on your lonely journey to becoming an accomplished writer. Look at Leonardo Da Vinci. The Renaissance genius filled hundreds of notebooks with his ideas, projects, sketches, and personal matters. His diaries were his life, and he wasn't seen anywhere without one. We can also learn how to use all the resources of our creative intelligence. How? By learning the seven creative principles stated by Da Vinci:

Curiositá: exploring reality, searching for continuous learning.

Dimostrazione: comparing knowledge and experience, learning from mistakes.

Sensazione: keeping your senses wide awake so you can live the experiences.

Sfumato: embracing ambiguity, paradoxical statements, and doubts.

Arte/scienza: keeping the balance between common sense and imagination, between art and science, between logic and absurd.

Corporalitá: keeping the balance between the body and the mind.

Connessione: acknowledging and appreciating the connectivity among all kinds of things.

Groovy Cool Writing Technique #17

COMPLETE LEONARDO'S NOTEBOOK. Da Vinci made the most of his notebooks as far as creativity is concerned. Those notebooks reflect his curiositá, which is indispensable for creating. He poured onto his pages all his continuous learning and also his sensazione, especially those provided by the sense of sight.

Here are some ideas to put into your own notebook:

Write the 100 most important questions to you. How can I make more money this year? How can I have more fun every Sunday? How can I lose 20 pounds without giving up chocolate? How can I sleep more and better? Why do I procrastinate every time I am going to write? Why do doorbells get on my nerves? Why do I never remember my dreams when I wake up? Now stop asking logical questions and start asking absurd ones, like how can I print documents without using any ink? How can I kiss my boss without him knowing that it is I who is kissing him?

Write 100 things you would like to do before you die. Stepping inside the Trevi Fountain; eat a hot dog under the Eiffel Tower on a night with a full moon; finish reading Ulysses by James Joyce, Marcel Proust, Hamlet; travel by hot-air balloon; publish some novels; travel to Africa and touch a giraffe...

Make a list of 100 entries that start with "I like" and another list that starts with "I don't like". Make each item as precise as possible. Don't write "I like flowers", but "I like wild flowers, especially if they are yellow and I pick them myself while I am walking in the forest". Make it personal. Don't write "I like sleeping without my pajamas", but "I like sleeping without my pajamas and watching my auntie's face when she catches me walking to the toilet, naked, in the middle of the night".

Make a list of 100 entries starting with "I remember..." and another starting with "I have forgotten..." Then write another list of 100 entries starting with "Always..." and another one starting with "Never..."

Chapter Thirteen

Why 100? This practice is based on the so-called Abundance Principle: more is never less; more is always more. The first 10 questions that you have written, or the first 10 items stating what you like, pop easily into your head; when you reach to number 35 or 40, you start writing more relevant topics, and when you near number 100, you discover unexpected, deep ideas.

Watch reality according to a certain topic. Choose a topic in the morning and watch things from that point of view for the rest of the day. For example: obedience. Through the day, write down everything that catches your attention about that topic in your diary. Remember: be precise. Obedience is my legs following my brain's expressed command to walk. My hand, while lighting a cigarette, disobeys my choice to quit smoking, although it obeys my desires at the same time. Obedience is the cars stopped at the traffic lights, and also the pedestrians crossing the road following the directions of the green light. Obedience is the military discipline of my co-worker. The sun obeys by shining every day. Have you seen that man who disobeys his turn and jumps the queue at the bakery?

CHAPTER FOURTEEN

What Is an Octopus Doing in a Garage? Writing from Objects.

For some authors, especially classical authors, objects we can find in our daily lives are essential for telling the stories. This was especially true for Gustave Flaubert, author of Madame Bovary. For him, everyday objects were of the utmost importance in creating stories. He used to claim that even the most familiar things gain an unbelievable power if we watch them carefully. Look around yourself. What can you see on your desk? A solar-powered calculator, a mobile phone, a cup of coffee or tea, a postcard pinned to your notice board, books, a box of biscuits, an electronic bullseye...

Madame Bovary is a very interesting book if you want to learn about characterization, especially in relation to the objects surrounding the characters. Flaubert structures his characters according to different objects that they possess: Charles' hat, Rodolphe's boots, Emma's wedding bouquet...

Those objects show Charles's boring personality, Rodolphe's seduction power, and the future of a marriage that is condemned to wither.

Good writers know that the setting is an essential part of the story, not only because of the frame that it offers, but also because the furniture, walls, and domestic objects can help to show the personality traits of every character. You can ask yourself: what does my character collect? For example, if I were writing about a nursery teacher, what would she store in her cupboards and drawers? Open possibilities. Unopened sugar packets? Porcelain owls? High-heel shoes? Novels with lots of typos? Or maybe she collects razors?

Not only do the characters possess objects, but objects also possess the characters, taking hold of their conflicts and problems, hiding their mysteries, and keeping or revealing their secrets. What if those unopened sugar packets reflect our teacher's tendency to deprive herself of the simple pleasures of life? Someone who collects sugar packets that have never been opened can also collect promising dates she never went to, laughs that never burst. In that way, the packets would symbolize the different life trains that the teacher missed and let go. What if the nursery teacher's sweetness is just the balance for a hidden and withdrawn violence, violence that can be dangerous if she ever finds out the way of letting it out, and that suppressed violence makes her collect razors?

Chapter Fourteen

In this chapter we are going to see how objects, beyond helping the reader to visualize the scene, can act as triggers during the first stages of creation, while we are still nursing creative ideas. How can they be triggers? We have to relieve them of their merely decorative role and transform them into passive subjects of our stories.

Groovy Cool Writing Technique #18

PLACE AN OCTOPUS IN A GARAGE. This is a creative game that consists in decontextualizing, in placing objects in unusual places.

First of all, make a list of ten objects:

olive

spoon

horseshoe

brush

handkerchief

measuring tape

sock

basket

stapler

pen

Now, make a list of ten places:

playground

deserted beach

disco

confession booth

bank

prison cell

museum

dressing room

cave

port

After you finish writing both lists, write questions by mixing elements from both lists: What the heck is a/an... doing in a/an...? For example, what the heck is a horseshoe doing in a dressing room? What the heck is a brush doing in a cave? Try to write plots that answer those questions.

What the heck is a measuring tape doing on a deserted beach? Maybe it belongs to some Robinson Crusoe wannabe who left it behind after trying to put together an Ikea hut. What the heck is a basket doing in a disco? Little Red Riding Hood forgot it there; she was going to her grandma's house, but she got sidetracked to go dancing with the wolf.

You can also play with the meanings that are most popularly associated to those objects. A horseshoe, in many different cultures, it is a good luck symbol. Maybe it is in a dressing room because the actor using that room is very superstitious and believes it will make him be successful on the opening night of his latest play.

Groovy Cool Writing Technique #19

MY TREASURE: FETISHES AND CHARMS. We consider a material object to be a fetish when we believe that it brings us good luck. For example, always wearing the same T-shirt when taking a test.

The dictionary defines amulet as an object that brings good luck while having some supernatural power. Remember The Neverending Story, by Michael Ende? Auryn was a medallion with two snakes that bite each other's tails on one side, and the sentence "Do what you wish" on the back. This medallion fulfills your dreams. Well, then why don't you look for either a fetish or an amulet for your main character? Why don't you give your character an object they cannot live without, like Linus van Pelt's blanket?

Think of objects that can be turned into fetishes and associate them with characters. A Madonna T-shirt that an uncomplaining mother of several children has carefully hidden among her clothes since she went to a concert when she was young and carefree? An eraser in the shape of a little dog that a university professor keeps since he was a child and needs to touch whenever he has to give a lecture?

Let's crown it all! What if that eraser is a magic charm? What if that eraser in the shape of a dog barks from the professor's pocket whenever he is threatened? What if that eraser can immediately erase all the mistakes he makes during his lectures?

Groovy Cool Writing Technique #20

I LIKE BEING A PAN, DON'T I? This game starts once more with a list of objects. You can use a dictionary to help you if you wish; in that way you won't mention just the things that you know and are familiar with. Choose a letter from the dictionary, open the dictionary and write the random words that appear on that page: funicular, florin, façade, food, floor, fact.

Now choose one of those words and put yourself in its shoes. I am a funicular. What do I like about being a funicular? What don't I like about being a funicular? I like it because I go from one place to the other, meeting different people. I don't like it because I don't like being always pulling a cable, but it's the price I have to pay for being able to move.

I am a florin and I like it because I am an ancient coin, one with lineage, so I am very expensive and valuable. But I don't like it because now I am a disused coin. Before, people were happy when they saw me, but once the Euro coin appeared, I said goodbye to both fame and reputation. At the same time, I like being kind of invisible, since it was exhausting to always go from hand to hand.

I am a facade and I like having so many eyes overlooking the street because I like watching. And I also like that people look at me. I don't like it when people pin notices and posters to me, or when they paint graffiti, or when it rains because I cannot see clearly.

CHAPTER FIFTEEN

That's All Folks! Or Maybe Not...

You start a story: your protagonist visits her husband in a hospital. She leaves too late so she misses the last train that would take her back home, where her disabled mother and two teenage children are waiting for her. What can she do? Will she spend the night on the platform? Will she go back to the hospital? Will she phone her only distant relative that lives in the city so she can spend the night with him? Will she catch another train whose destination is unknown to her?

Most of the creative writing techniques we have explained here dealt with the beginnings and the triggers of the stories. Now, we are going to create stories starting by their endings.

Let's go back to the previous example. You have thought of a trigger for a story: a woman misses her train. What would happen if we make that fact the ending of the story instead of the trigger? I will write a story whose ending is a woman who misses a train, so she decides to take another one to an unknown destination, thus abandoning everything contained in her world: husband, teenaged children, elderly mother... A woman who steps away from her self-sacrificing life, not voluntarily, but because she misses that train. That little mistake gives her the courage she needed to do what she wouldn't have ever done otherwise: quitting everything and starting a new life from scratch.

How can we bring the reader to that final scene, made up by us beforehand? That will be a creative challenge and a great exercise in planning — highly recommended to all those pantsers out there (yeah, me included), all those writers who prefer to see their stories grow by mere improvisation.

Improvisation doesn't work with the game of the endings!

You have to get to that train, to that train station, to the protagonist's dream, in the most coherent, authentic, realistic, inevitable, and surprising way possible. Ideas? Every single one that may pop into your mind: she discovered that her husband was cheating on her thanks to a phone call to her husband's mobile phone while he was sleeping; one of her teenaged sons has stolen the money she had saved to buy drugs, and now she is scared to go back home in case he threatens her for more money; both her husband and her mother have verbally abused her for years despite her self-sacrifice, and she had never complained until today; she has been looking through a travel brochure at the hospital; she had a dream about her first love, who lives in Australia now...

Write down as many ideas that you can come up with as quickly as you can. But remember that all of them must point to that predetermined chosen destination.

So let's write starting from an ending:

Exact endings: throw ideas for endings that imply a creative challenge because it seems difficult to imagine how the main character can get there. It helps to think about the last shot in a film:

A man gets out of the bus, takes his shoes off in the middle of the street, throws them into a litter bin, and walks away barefoot.

A girl throws a colander into the family swimming pool and, without a flinch, watches it sink.

A woman writes "Thank you, life" on her Twitter account and then she empties the whole magazine of her gun.

A man opens a suitcase that contains bundles of $500 notes and then throws all the money into the sea.

General endings: write down purposes. The important thing is not that you know now the details of those endings, but to know what you want to achieve with them.

At the end, my protagonist learns how to say no to others' demands.

At the end, my protagonist, who has always been discriminated against and undervalued, gets acknowledgement for a task he performed.

At the end, my protagonist, whose life was miserable and resentful, manages to forgive.

At the end, my very individualistic protagonist, finds happiness by helping others in an altruistic way.

At the end, my protagonist finally gets the woman he wants, just to discover that he doesn't love her after all.

Changing the endings! Play with the endings of your favorite novels and films. For example, Thelma and Louise both turn themselves in to the police instead of driving off the cliff. In Gran Torino the protagonist isn't murdered.

Remember: by changing the endings, you are also changing the beginning! What things from the original story must you change to make the ending contrary to the original? Will you change the personality traits of the characters, the circumstances, the facts?

Exact meanings can give you many opportunities to use your imagination: what happened to that man who decided to take his shoes off when he got off the bus and dump them in the bin before walking away barefoot? Maybe those were new shoes and they were hurting his feet. Maybe those painful shoes are symbols of the oppression he had to endure from his employer, who fired him today. Maybe walking barefoot along the streets symbolizes trusting in life, having hope for the future.

Why does a man throw a whole suitcase of money into the sea? Is he nuts? Is it fake money? Is the money a prop for a play about gangsters that has just been suspended because the company doesn't have enough money to rent the theatre? Is he an actor in an advert for perfume for the men of today?

General endings start from the conclusions, so we can make up the premises later. At the end of your story, your main character will have learnt to say no: to the telemarketer trying to sell a new mobile phone; to a husband whom she despises; to her daughters, who take advantage of her by making her take care of the grandchildren on a daily basis...

What will motivate that change? How is that change going to happen? Something will have an influence on her: an illness, or a new friend who is more independent than herself, or her late discovery that she loves the written word, or a secret love...

The change will need to happen gradually; we will change it scene by scene, one step at a time, until the ending we reach for becomes believable: the transformation experienced by a woman, who stops being passive and starts acknowledging what she wants, who knows when to say no.

Groovy Cool Writing Technique #21

THAT'S ALL, FOLKS? NO, IT'S JUST THE BEGINNING! Try it now. Think of a final scene that is surprising and unexpected for your story. Next imagine characters, scenes and dialogues that make it possible to reach that ending. You will then have to write the story in a chronological order and, even though you already know the ending, you have to try not to reveal it to your readers until the last. Only when they finish reading the story will the readers understand why you chose that ending and how you got there.

AFTERWORD

Sparks to flame —

From idea to product is a long road

"... nobody said that this was going to be easy." — Cinta Garcia de la Rosa, Creative Writing Techniques.

Creating is work. It can be invigorating, exciting, exhilarating — like a good workout or a thrill ride. And like exercise and thrills, creating consumes energy and time.

One of the most important points that Ms. Garcia has made in this guide is that your creativity begins working on your story or novel long before you put that first word onto the page or the screen. It's at work deep in your subconscious while you're strolling through the park, riding the metro, even while you're sleeping. Your creativity makes connections while your conscious mind isn't aware of it.

And that's work, too. In this book, Cinta has given us invaluable ideas and illustrated them with some of the most creative, wonderful examples I have ever read. It's up to us now to put those techniques and those ideas to work for ourselves.

Pick up the hammer

It's one thing to think of a great opening or a cool ending to a story. Taking your reader from the beginning to the end, making sure they always want to read the next word, is a long and difficult journey.

This book is replete with good advice to help your readers make that trip. As Cinta explains in Chapter 10, "In People's Shoes. If You Want to Write, Empathize!" you need to get to know your characters: what do they think about abstract concepts like honesty and ethics? How would they react in a situation? What's their back-story, their history, their reasons for acting the way they do? What do they think while they're doing it?

And you need to know your plot, firmly and completely. I don't believe in "writing by the seat of your pants." As an author, you need to have clear in your own mind at least a basic story arc. Sure, your characters may surprise you by acting in ways you hadn't foreseen, but that just means that you're both more imaginative and observant than you gave yourself credit for.

A plot outline that makes sense will save you a lot of time and give you a story that works, one that's believable and interesting — one that your readers will stay with to the end.

I have tried writing from an interesting opening scene or line without a clear idea of where I wanted to go. All I got after hours and days of writing were pages of prose that I had no more interest in. When the author is bored with a story, there's just no rescuing it.

Finished the draft? Great — now, you can start working

The author's job doesn't end when you first type "The End." Those words only mean that now you have some raw material to work with — ore from which to extract precious elements, rough stones to chip polish into gems. If you're like most professional writers, you'll probably spend more time reading, rewriting, re-reading and rewriting your story again.

But don't try to do it yourself. Writing may be a solitary art, but publishing is a team sport. Share your work with "beta readers" — independent people who will give you honest feedback about your writing. Don't depend on your family and friends to evaluate your story. They're probably more interested in preserving your friendship than in telling you that you have a lot more work to do before your manuscript is ready for the world. The bastards.

Of course, when you ask someone to review your work, it only makes sense to respond to their concerns. Plug the plot holes, correct the inconsistencies, clear up the confusion. You don't have to do everything that your beta readers ask for, but you do need to take their comments seriously. If there's something they don't understand, it's a weakness that you, the creator of this work of literary art, have to fix.

Don't try this alone

After you fix the problems your beta readers found, you need to re-read and re-edit your manuscript again. Then it might be ready for a professional editor.

"Editing" is actually a broad term that encompasses several similar, yet distinct operations.

Substantive editing is a look at the overall structure of the book: is it complete? Does it answer all the questions it poses, or at least attempt to? Does it pull the reader from beginning to end? Does it make sense? Are the characters sympathetic, or at least interesting? Are they flat, cut-out figures repeating lines that other writers have put into their books a thousand times before?

Copy-editing is a closer look at the mechanics of writing. The copy-editor will find grammatical and spelling mistakes, will advise you to change passive voice to active, change noun phrases to verbs, reduce the number of adjectives and adverbs, tell you that you wrote "affect" when you should have used "effect," and so on.

Do what the copy-editor says.

Then go through your manuscript one more time. No one is perfect, not even copy-editors, and you'll find more errors now that you're sensitized to your own weaknesses.

If you can afford it, you should have the copy-editor read your manuscript again, after your corrections. It will amaze you how many little, obvious mistakes you will find in your manuscript after you're sure that you've checked it carefully.

Proofreading used to mean ensuring that the typeset book matched the typed manuscript — back in the days when typesetters would produce galleys from the author's manuscript. Now that we go from computer file directly to e-book, there's theoretically no reason for sections of the story to be missing from the final product — but that still happens.

Today, proofreading is a last careful look at spelling, punctuation and completeness. A good proofreader will find where words, sentences and paragraphs got inadvertently deleted in one of the previous editing phases.

All these are distinct skills, and a good substantive editor is not necessarily a good proofreader. Nor vice-versa.

Look for qualified people for each of these stages. They're worth it. Remember, no one can do all these things. Least of all the author. You cannot proofread your own writing, because you when you read your own work, you don't see what's actually on the page — you see what you intended to write.

Am I discouraging you?

It's hard work, and it's rewarding. When the words flow through your mind faster than you can type them, when the pages fill up before your eyes — that's rewarding like nothing else in the world. But writing for an audience of strangers, writing work that strangers will want to read, is a lot of hard work. Get others involved to help you, and keep going. Because there's nothing like holding a book that has your name on the cover.

It's a long journey. Start now.

I'd like to end this afterword with a message to the author of the book proper: Cinta, all of us who have read this guidebook now want to read those stories you have tantalized us with — the retired pickpocket, the woman on the wrong train, the evil muse in the pen. We can't wait to read them in your inimitable style!

— Scott Bury, 2014

ABOUT THE AUTHOR

Cinta Garcia de la Rosa is an International Award-Winning Author who spends her time in the United States and Spain with her amazing husband. Along with writing, her career encompasses beta-reading, editing, proofreading, and translating Spanish/English. Cinta has loved the written word since she was five years old and reads at least one hundred books every year. She has a B.A. in English with minors in Literature, Art, and Creative Writing from Oxford. Cinta has published:

A Foreigner in London (included in the anthology Blessings from the Darkness).

Never Again (included in the anthology Satan's Holiday, and written under the pen name Rosa Storm).

The Funny Adventures of Little Nani, Book One (Children's Book), a Gold Medal Winner in the Children's category of the International Readers' Favorite Book Awards.

Deadly Company (included in the anthology Don't

Look Back: Thirteen Terrifying Tales of Urban Folklore, and written under the pen name Rosa Storm).

You can follow her writing adventures by signing up to her newsletter: http://eepurl.com/XFVwT

If you want to interact with her, you can follow her in the following social media links:

Twitter: https://twitter.com/CintaNani78

Facebook: https://www.facebook.com/pages/Cinta-Garcia-de-la-Rosa/333755993341596

Blog: http://cintascorner.com

Website: http://cintagarcia.com

ΠOTE TO THE REΛDER

Being an Indie Author, the participation of the readers in the process of marketing a book is essential. Please, either if you like this book or not, take a few minutes to go to Amazon and post a review. Reviews are extremely helpful and make us gain visibility. So if you are going to post a review, thank you. If you decide not to post the review, thanks anyways, because at least you read my book. But I love reviews! So please consider writing one.

Printed in Great Britain
by Amazon

87218041R00068